Business Survival
For Project Management

**Business
Survival**

**Learning and implementing project
management best practices is essential
for business survival!**

The Vision Tree, Ltd.   Claudia J. Pannell

This publication is designed to provide accurate and authoritative information in regard to the subject matter covered. It is sold with the understanding that the publisher is not engaged in rendering legal, accounting, or other professional services. If legal advice or other expert assistance is required, the services of a competent professional should be sought.

Editorial Assistant: Barbara L. Coffing
Cover Design: Joanne Osmond
Copyright © 2009 by Claudia J. Pannell, MBA, PMP (2004-2006)

Published by The Vision Tree, Ltd.
216 Waterbury Circle, Lake Villa, IL 60046 USA
Survival@TheVisionTree.com
847.356.7550 Fax: 847.356.3783

Printed in the United States of America
ISBN: 978-1-933334-16-5

Acknowledgement

This book is dedicated to my husband, Larry Pannell and my father, Howard Gatewood. They are the two most important men in my life and always continue to support me in my desire to learn and share my life experiences.

Many people in my life have encouraged me and I will be forever grateful for their mentoring, patience, and understanding. They have never given up on me and always challenged me to take the first step whether it is continued education, a challenging project or an unproven idea! You know how you are, but among the first supporters of this endeavor were Jeni, Joanne, Barb, Jim, Randy and my awesome Mother-in-Law, Wynell. Most endearing are all of my First Saturday friends. They allowed me to pitch my ideas and returned the favor with honest feedback that helps me continue to improve and expand the bounds of my creativity. Thanks to each of you – Mary and Kevin, Cynthia and Damon, Michael and Andi, Kim and Bill, Dana and Chuck!

Table of Contents

Knowledge Areas And Process Groups

Knowledge Area and Process Groups

This book and game are based on A Guide to the Project Management Book of Knowledge (PMBOK® Guide, 2000 Edition and Third Edition), and questions similar to those which may be expected for PMP® Certification. Knowing and understanding all the correct answers to these questions does not constitute a guarantee to pass the PMP® Exam.

Project Management Best Practices

A good Project Manager is sought after for their knowledge, their expertise and their commitment to see projects through successfully. A poor Project Manager is like a hot potato...business cannot get rid of them soon enough! But the best Project Managers are those who can adapt quickly, know, and understand the business for which a project is being undertaken, and have the ability to relate positively to those they interact with on a given project.

Emerson once said, "The ability to create is the ability to adapt." That statement could not be truer about Project Managers. It is also true that adaptability spawns creativity. Those who have learned to adapt quickly by keeping their focus on the road ahead are also the ones who are the most successful.

Six Honest Serving Men
From *The Elephant's Child*
By Rudyard Kipling

I keep six honest serving men
(They taught me all I knew);
Their names are What and Why and When
And How and Where and Who

These four simple lines can be applied to project management. Following the logic that adaptability and creativity go hand-in-hand, expand these statements to help think out-of-the-box for guidance during projects.

What?

In the Planning Process Group and Cost Knowledge Area, a project manager should ask questions like, "what is needed for additional project resources?" They should also consider what human resources are required or what estimate and budget resources should be considered in this project?

A project manager should ask, "What techniques or methods are available to use?" If they are available, have they been proven or is their use on this project, the first? Can this project afford to be the first to use these techniques or methods? From a project quality perspective, are these techniques or methods reasonable and practical in this business environment?

When considering Time in the Planning Process group, project managers should consider the best way to organize the activities of the project. What is the first step? What is the last step? What steps are contingent on others? Can any steps be omitted? Have you considered the process steps from every organization involved in the project?

In Project Control, when a project manager is considering Integrated Change Control, it may be a good idea to bring the project team together and ask, "Can this project (or idea or concept) be better?" This is not to say one should second-guess the project. It is simply to point out, it is never a bad time to consider if the project still meets the requirements of the business. Best practices would encourage periodic "time-outs" for this kind of review. Adjustments should be made, even if it means canceling a project to align with changing business initiatives.

Why?

Generally speaking, when the concept for the project is relayed to a project manager, the project manager can grasp the idea and capture the fundamentals in their project charter. However, there are times when project managers are faced with a project where it just does not pass the logic test. In other words, it is difficult for the project manager to understand the reason for doing the project in the first place. If the project manager cannot understand the purpose of the project, they will have a difficult time convincing team members, vendors, clients, management or any other stakeholders on why resources should be invested in the project.

At times like this, project managers should expect to spend a great deal of time in research. That research can and should be anything from how the project idea was conceived to the expected outcome and the known benefactors. The most challenging part will be to understand the business associated with the project if the project manager is not educated or skilled in that area. For example, a project manager with an education and skills in business strategy may be able to quickly respond to issues related to Human Resources and Communications, but may be hesitant to assist in the area of source selection and contract administration when the project is creating a new design element for the engineers in manufacturing. They also may be able to give a broad answer to why this project is important, but will be hard-pressed to respond in detail to engineers that may oppose the new design element. It is for this reason, the best project managers have a thorough understanding, recent experience and a working knowledge of the business to which the project is related.

With this background, a project manager will consider questions like, "Why should anyone buy this idea?" This is a good question when Communication Planning is being addressed. Project Managers will also want to consider why the proposed way is better than any other way and address the answer in the Project Plan Development phase. The feasibility study will most likely have covered the question and if not, project managers should return to the initiation process and address it. During the Risk Identification process and Risk Planning steps, project managers should consider why resistance to the idea is so strong and how they will address any resistance. For example, will a plan for mitigation be developed or will the issue be the basis for a recommendation for not pursuing the project?

When?

In some situations a project manager may be the originator of the project idea. Whether they are or not, there are a few questions under the heading of "when", which should be considered so as to be prepared in the event they should present themselves.

For example, during the feasibility study, or the Scope Planning and Communication Planning processes, a project manager should ask, "When should I introduce the plan?" Here the "plan" is the idea or concept for a project. "When should you implement the plan?" A project manager will look closely at the Time Planning process and the Schedule Development process to make sure the optimal implementation time is selected. Since environmental, seasonal, or business effects could influence the plan, close scrutiny is warranted.

Often, a critical question that is delayed or never asked is, "When should the strategy of the plan be revised?" Project managers and team members may think that the cancellation or change in direction of a project is the result of poor management. In fact, the opposite is more likely to be true. Project managers with their finger on the pulse of the business situation and control of a project, often are the first to recognize when a project will no longer meet the needs of the business. They are aware of the long-term objectives and can provide insight and advise management to consider cutting losses in favor of moving resources to prepare for a change coming to the business environment.

Project managers are often faced with questioning a change in strategy during the schedule control process and from feedback received when executing communications. It is critical they stay focused on what is best for the business, not necessarily what is best for the project. Projects come and go, but it is the business that fuels the need for projects in the first place. Project managers will be remembered for the value they brought to the business.

How?

Project managers and the rest of a project team are likely to ask how they are doing. The Quality knowledge area is where we find these kinds of questions being asked. But these are not the only "How" questions. For example, "How can we improve on the project?" For this question, project managers look to the Executing process and their Quality Assurance area. They will also find answers in the Control process with Quality Control. Additionally, Scope, Scheduling, Cost, Performance, and Risk Monitoring and Control are areas that will provide good insight on how to improve.

"How can we test the waters?" Project managers have found that pilots or proof-of-concept tasks performed during a feasibility study are a viable means to see if the product or service idea can survive. During the Initiating process, the feasibility study is often enlightening and can go a long way in either providing a strong foundation for the plan or suggesting another time or place would make a wiser choice. Sometimes, ideas are ahead of their time or past their prime. That does not mean they should be tossed away. It may only means there is an opportunity to improve on what has already been done. If this is the case, simply return to the question above, "How can we improve on the project or idea?"

Another interesting question is "How can I persuade the centers of influence?" Many times a great idea or concept never gets off the ground because the owner simply did not have the skills or the knowledge necessary to "sell" their idea. The truth may be simpler than one would think.

During the Initiating process, a project manager may find it an interesting exercise to determine the "WIIFM" from the perspective of the recipient of the product or service. WIIFM means "what's in it for me". Therefore, the project manager puts on the hat of the recipient and by reversing roles, looks for the benefits.

The benefits may not be enough. Another good practice is to "follow the money". By using Earned Value Management (EVM), a project manager can display control at every aspect of the project. Giving examples of past projects utilizing EVM can demonstrate a project manager's ability to deliver on time, within budget and with high quality. Centers of influence will find this helpful when considering a future project for a product or service. This is because many businesses make decisions based on the concept that past behavior is a good indicator of future behavior (although not a good idea if you are considering financial investments!).

Where?

A novice project manager often struggles with knowing where to start. Good project management never has one guessing. Project Initiating leads one through the steps that get a project started. Once the Project Charter is complete and a Project Manager is assigned, there should be enough data to start work on the project scope. With the help of historic data and common tips and tricks, a project manager is past the start and embarking on the project planning.

Another good "where" question to ask is "Where is resistance likely to be found?" Project managers address this question during the Risk Management Planning. They will identify the risk (i.e., resistance to project product or service), perform a qualitative and quantitative risk analysis and provide a risk response. In this way, they will be prepared to meet the resistance and mitigate it, with any luck, to the satisfaction of those resisting the project product or service.

"Where should I plant the seeds?" Whether it is an idea or concept to be launched, or a project manager just looking for a support network, Communication Planning is the place to be. During the Initiating process, specifically the feasibility study, a project manager is going to be looking to see who stands to gain the most benefit from the product or service. This information will be translated later in the communications to focus on the benefits to the audience.

Who?

There are many "who's" in most projects especially the complex ones. However, there are four specific "who" questions a project manager will definitely want to consider.

First, "Who can help or make contributions to this project product or service?" Besides the project manager, the management sponsor and the core project team, a project manager is going to analyze the Human Resource Plan and scrutinize the Team Development during execution to make sure the correct individuals are on the project. The project manager will also be concerned with other stakeholders such as the customers and the vendors. When looking for help and positive contributions to the project, it is important to take into consideration the feedback of customers during a feasibility study and the comments expressed by potential business partners during the vendor selection process.

Whether it is for financial backing, personal support, team morale, or customer purchases, a project manager is always keeping an eye on "who" their target audience will be. Sometimes the answers are found during the Initiating processes, specifically in identifying the business objectives. The answer may be the same for all audiences, but the delivery may need to be tweaked to be more personal and again answers the question, "what is in it for me" from the reader's perspective.

As a project manager proceeds through the project, it may become evident that additional resources will be required. At the beginning of a project, a project manager will better be able to respond to situations like this, if they prepare their stakeholders for a worse case scenario. Then, if the time should come, there are no surprises. So, in the planning process during risk analysis, this should be a consideration. Additionally, the cost planning and procurement planning processes will want to consider the potential future needs of this scenario. A "heads-up" to the contact administration team will help eliminate hurdles at a time when speed can be of the essence. It should be noted here, however, that project managers need to be very conscientious about avoiding the urge to "pad" the picture. This is a time when very good estimating is essential. Paint a true picture of the best, worse and most likely events. Your stakeholders will remember this as a positive reflection and it paves to way to trusting relationships.

The final "who" question has already been asked in a variety of ways. Perhaps that is the point and why it is still a very important question to ask. "Who will benefit?" Good project management would say this is the project's mantra and should be kept visible for all the team to see. The point is, if the deliverables of the project are of no benefit to anyone, the team is working on a doomed project. Therefore, it is essential that during the Initiating process, the product or service description must clearly state the benefits and to whom they will be bestowed.

What, Why, When, How, Where & Who?

We have taken a look at six important categories of questions that project managers might use as they proceed through their projects. These are useful questions and some are often forgotten. But the purpose here is to help create a safety net of sorts that can be easily remembered and gives good reference points when working with the process groups and knowledge areas of the PMBOK®.

On the following pages, are some good tips, tricks, and memory strategies that may be helpful in studying for the PMP® Exam.

Enjoy and Good Luck!

Show me and I forget;

Tell me and I remember;

Involve me and I understand!

Author Unknown

Reinforced Learning

Reinforced Learning

If you have never created or used a memory map, it is a good idea to start now. Many of the PMP® prep courses, classes and instructors will advise you to do a "mind dump" before you begin the exam. That is a good description of a memory map!

As you prepare for the PMP® Exam, you will have the opportunity to spend a few moments before the exam begins to gather your thoughts. It is during this time that you will want to put down, on the paper given to you by the test center, as much as you can to help you answer questions quickly.

Understanding the order (inputs/outputs, tools and techniques) of the knowledge areas and process groups is critical. So is the variety of formulas, ratios and variances used in project management. A memory map is an organized way to provide this highly detailed and often complex information in a shorthand method. Using (sometimes "senseless") acronyms will further this process.

Following are several topics provided in one example of a memory map that may be helpful. After creating the memory map over and over until it becomes very easy to create, you should time yourself to make sure you can create it in a minimum of 5 minutes. That is all the time you should allow for this exercise during the exam.

Initiating & Planning

Initiating is the first area of the memory map and we will be combining it with the second area, Planning. The acronym for Initiating and Planning will be:

S O I C P

This acronym will be read as:

Soon

Our

Ideas

Can

Progress

This acronym may help you remember the following tasks and process groups in the proper order:

Feasibility Study

Business Objective

Product / Service Description

Initiating

Project Charter

Project Manager Assigned

The underlined words in the acronym correlate to the underlined words of the tasks and process groups. At first glance it may appear confusing as to why the first letters of the words in the tasks and process groups are not always used. This is because the memory map utilizes a diagramed visual approach. This will make more sense as we explain the memory map.

When writing this information on the memory map in a timed environment, it is natural to want to abbreviate words and phrases. Below is a sample of how the above information could be documented on the memory map.

① INITIATION / PLANNING (SOICP)

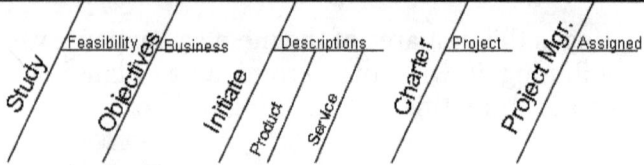

* For the purposes of these exercises, the illustrations will be numbered to help identify where they go on the finished memory map.

When creating a memory map, use as few words as possible without loosing the meaning of the topics. For example, in the above information, think of the following as you are writing:

The first stage is Initiation and consists of:

A study. (what kind of study? Feasibility)

Therefore, the important word is STUDY and a descriptive of that word is FEASIBILITY.

The next content of Initiation is:

Objectives (what kind of objectives? Business)

Again the important word here is OBJECTIVES and a description of that word is BUSINESS.

In the third content of Initiation, there is a small difference. The important word is INITIATE. What do you want to initiate? DESCRIPTIONS of PRODUCTS and SERVICES.

By now you can probably get a feel for writing the memory map, so you can see how the final two contents of Initiation are identified in the diagram. As you practice writing the map, over and over, within the time limit, it not only gets easier to create, but you will find that you can put a lot of valuable information in a comparatively small space. That is the secret to memory maps!

PRACTICE MAKES PERFECT!

Take time now to practicing your mapping techniques. Copy the above map over multiple times until you can recreate it without looking at it in the book or at the one you previously drew.

PRACTICE MAKES PERFECT!

Executing

The next area of the memory map is the Executing process group. As you might expect, this area is longer and more complex. The information is designed to help you remember the high points and to trigger your memory for the points in between.

Executing processes will be remembered with this acronym:

P Q T I S S C

The acronym stands for:

Presently

Queen

Tess

Is

So

Sincerely

Confident

The associated tasks for the Executing process group for this acronym are:

Project Plan Execution (which produces)

> Work Results; and

> Change Requests

Quality Assurance (which produces)

> Quality Improvements

Team Development (which produces)

> Performance Improvements

Information Distribution (which produces)

> Records;

> Reports; and

> Presentations

Sellers (which produces)

> Responses

Selection (which produces)

> Contracts

Contract Administration (which produces)

> Contract Changes; and

> Contract Closure

For the memory map and in an abbreviated style, you might see the Executing area as follows:

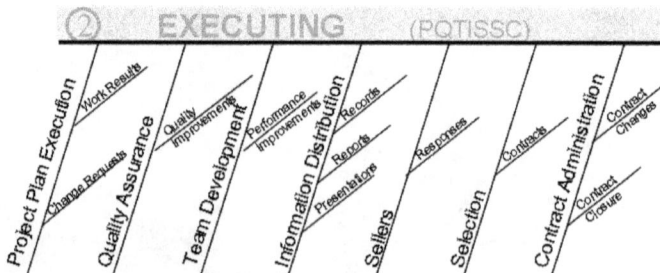

PRACTICE MAKES PERFECT!

Take time now to practicing your mapping techniques. Copy the above map over multiple times until you can recreate it without looking at it in the book or at the one you previously drew.

PRACTICE MAKES PERFECT!

Control

The Control Process will be diagrammed a little differently. What we want to demonstrate are the work results. The acronym for Control is:

Q P S

The acronym stands for:

Queens

Prefer

Strength

The format for this process will be documented in the following manner:

Quality (which consists of)

Control (which produces)

Quality Improvements

Performance Reporting (from Work Results and produces)

Performance Improvements; and

Change Control

Schedule / Scope / Cost Controls (which

produces)

Schedule / Scope / Cost Updates

Integrated Change Control; and

Risk Management and Control

Scope Verification (which produces)

Formal Acceptance

For the purposes of the memory map, the Control process will be charted as follows:

③ CONTROL (QPS)

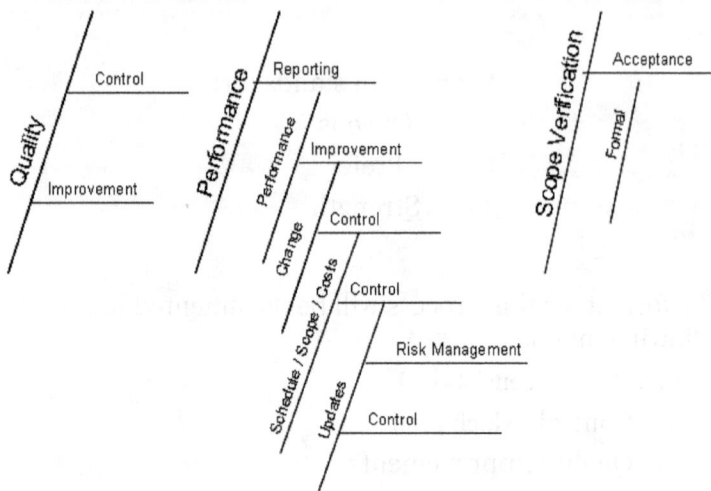

Quality
- Control
- Improvement

Performance
- Reporting
- Performance
  - Improvement
- Change
  - Control
- Schedule / Scope / Costs
  - Control
  - Updates
    - Risk Management
    - Control

Scope Verification
- Acceptance
- Formal

PRACTICE MAKES PERFECT!

Take time now to practicing your mapping techniques. Copy the above map over multiple times until you can recreate it without looking at it in the book or at the one you previously drew.

PRACTICE MAKES PERFECT!

Closure

The last process group to diagram will be the Closure group. There are two acronyms for this group and they will be identified as follows:

P P L P

These acronyms stand for the following:

Pretty

Polly

Liked

Parties

The best way to remember the tasks associated with Closure is to remember the paperwork. Documentation is closely associated with Closure, which is shown as follows:

Product Documentation (which produces)

      Administrative Closing

Project Archives

Lessons Learned

Project Closure (which produces)

      Contract

            Documentation, and

            Close Out

      Formal

            Approval, and

            Closure

Closing will be formatted on the memory map in the following way:

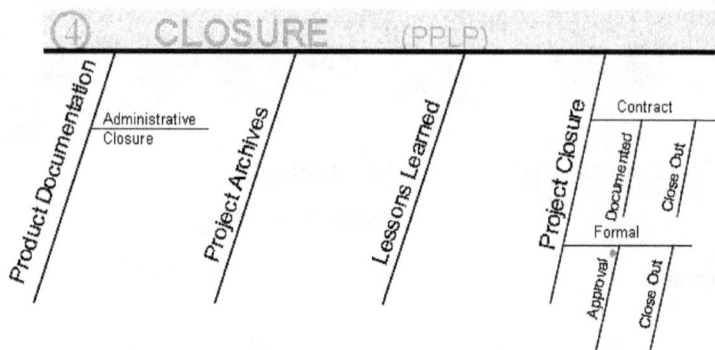

CLOSURE (PPLP)

- Product Documentation
  - Administrative Closure
- Project Archives
- Lessons Learned
- Project Closure
  - Contract
    - Documented
    - Close Out
  - Formal
    - Approval
    - Close Out

PRACTICE MAKES PERFECT!

Take time now to practicing your mapping techniques. Copy the above map over multiple times until you can recreate it without looking at it in the book or at the one you previously drew.

PRACTICE MAKES PERFECT!

Normal Distribution

A simple, but often omitted part of the understanding of project management is the normal distribution used to determine probability statistics. For the purpose of studying to pass the PMP® Exam, you only need the following:

One standard deviation from the mean in a normal distribution is 68.22% of the total population of the statistic being measured. Two standard deviations from the mean is 94.56% of the total. Three standard deviations from the mean is 99.73% and six standard deviations from the mean is 99.99% of the total population for the statistic being measured.

This tip will be displayed on the memory map in the following way:

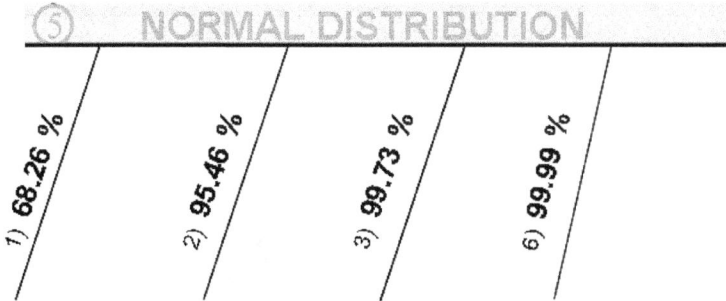

⑤ NORMAL DISTRIBUTION

1) 68.26 %
2) 95.46 %
3) 99.73 %
6) 99.99 %

PRACTICE MAKES PERFECT!

Take time now to practicing your mapping techniques. Copy the above map over multiple times until you can recreate it without looking at it in the book or at the one you previously drew.

PRACTICE MAKES PERFECT!

Ratios, Indices and Variance

Here we want to document the importance of the results of formulas being used throughout a project's life cycle. For example, ratios and indices, which are greater than one, are "good" while those, which are lesser than one, are "bad". Any that are equal to one are "on target".

In much the same way, variances that result in a negative number are "bad" and those that result in a positive number are "good". A variance that equals zero is "on target".

This concept will be documented on the memory map in the following way:

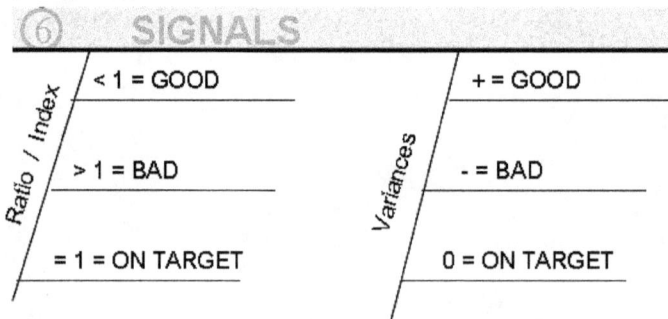

⑥ SIGNALS

Ratio / Index

< 1 = GOOD

> 1 = BAD

= 1 = ON TARGET

Variances

+ = GOOD

- = BAD

0 = ON TARGET

PRACTICE MAKES PERFECT!

Take time now to practicing your mapping techniques. Copy the above map over multiple times until you can recreate it without looking at it in the book or at the one you previously drew.

PRACTICE MAKES PERFECT!

More Formulas!

There are six additional formulas which should be given careful consideration in studying for the PMP® Exam. The first four pertain to the task of estimating activity durations. First is the PERT estimating formula. PERT stands for the Program Evaluation and Review Technique and is used in estimating the duration of task activities. There are three parts to the formula; the pessimistic estimate (P), the optimistic estimate (O) and the most likely estimate (M). The formula is calculated as the sum of the pessimistic estimate plus four times the most likely estimate plus the optimistic estimate. The result is divided by six. It is written as:

$$[P + 4(M) + O] / 6$$

The next formula is the Standard Deviation. This formula subtracts the optimistic estimate from the pessimistic estimate and divides the result by 6. It is written as:

$$[P - O] / 6$$

The third formula is the Task Variance and simply squares the result of the Standard Deviation. The formula is written as:

$$([P - O] / 6)^2$$

The next formula is calculating the Project Standard Deviation. For this formula, take the square root of the sum of the Task Variances. The formula is written as:

$$\sqrt{\text{Sum Task Var}}$$

The fifth formula is important in calculating the number of communication channels that will be used during a project. This formula calls for the number of stakeholders times the result of the number of stakeholders minus one. This result is then divided by two to arrive at how many communication channels are in the project. The formula is written as:

$$[N(N-1)] / 2$$

The final formula relates to the future value of money. Generally speaking, the future value of a sum of money is calculated by crediting and re-investing the interest on the money at the end of each year the money remains invested or utilized. The formula contains four variables which are:

FV = Future Value

PV = Present Value

r= rate of interest

n= number of time periods (usually years)

The formula is written as:

$$FV = PV / (1 + r)^n$$

For the memory map, the above six formulas will be documented as:

⑦ MATH

Formulas

$$PERT = \frac{P + 4M + O}{6}$$

$$Task\ Var = \left(\frac{P - O}{6}\right)^2$$

$$Std\ Dev = \frac{P - O}{6}$$

$$Proj\ Std\ Dev = \sqrt{Sum\ Task\ Var}$$

$$Communication\ Channels = \frac{N(N-1)}{2}$$

$$Future\ Value = \frac{PV}{(1 - r)^2}$$

PRACTICE MAKES PERFECT!

Take time now to practicing your mapping techniques. Copy the above map over multiple times until you can recreate it without looking at it in the book or at the one you previously drew.

PRACTICE MAKES PERFECT!

Common Tools and Techniques

When considering all the necessary items a project manager has at their disposal, it is often a good idea to remember them as the common tools and techniques. For the memory map, use the acronym:

S T A M P E D

This is translated as:

S = Systems, Software and Skills
T = Templates
A = Analysis and Audits
M = Meetings and Metrics
P = Performance Measures
E = EVA and Expert Judgment
D = Diagrams and Decision Points

This acronym will be documented in the memory map as follows:

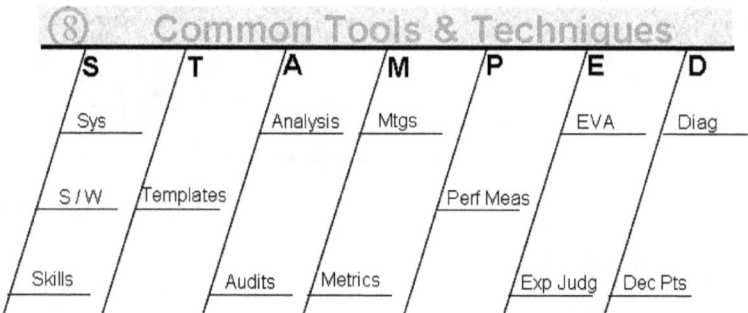

⑧ Common Tools & Techniques

S	T	A	M	P	E	D
Sys		Analysis	Mtgs		EVA	Diag
S/W	Templates			Perf Meas		
Skills		Audits	Metrics		Exp Judg	Dec Pts

PRACTICE MAKES PERFECT!

Take time now to practicing your mapping techniques. Copy the above map over multiple times until you can recreate it without looking at it in the book or at the one you previously drew.

PRACTICE MAKES PERFECT!

Earned Value Analysis

Before we get into a discussion about more formulas, let me share the following with you.   With a little imagination, this story can be converted to help memorize important formulas.

* * * * * *

Every year the automotive industry looks to improve the safety and appeal of its products. Did you know that they always have several EXPERIMENTAL VEHICLES they send BACK to the factory to COMPLETE A PORTION of the design improvements after the public has seen the originals?

EV = BAC * %COMP

For example, they have had some COMMERCIAL VEHICLES that started out as EXPERIMENTS without AIR CONDITIONING.

CV = EV – AC

They also have had some SPORT VEHICLES that began as EXPERIMENTS without any extra components found in PUBLIC VEHICLES, like fare meters.

SV = EV – PV

Many of the vehicles contained special monitoring devices such as the CRASH POSITION INDICATOR which compiled crash information and was divided into two groups – information from the EXPERIMENTAL VEHICLES and information from experimental vehicles without AIR CONDITIONING.

$$CPI = EV / AC$$

Another special device was the SMART PLUG-INS. These devices were divided up among the EXPERIMENTAL VEHICLES and the PUBLIC VEHICLES such as buses and taxis.

$$SPI = EV / PV$$

Since the environmental effects from vehicles are always a concern, the industry added an electronic air cleaner to the vehicles with AIR CONDITIONING to determine what PERCENT of the air was being COMPLETELY cleaned of any pollutants.

$$EAC = AC / \%COMP$$

As good as that sounds, the ENVIRONMENTAL TECHNOLOGY CENTER required the industry to test the electronic air cleaner in each vehicle without consideration to an AIR CONDITIONER.

$$ETC = EAC - AC$$

As a result, the industry created a **VOLUNTARY ACTION COMMITTEE** to go **BACK** and test all vehicles without the **ELECTRONIC AIR CLEANER**. This provided a starting point to judge their progress.

$$VAC = BAC - EAC$$

* * * * * *

Read the story a second and third time until you have it memorized. Use the formulas as your outline. For example, as you read the first paragraph, write out the formula that follows it below the paragraph. The formula abbreviations are coordinated with the corresponding story element (**ALL BOLDED**) to help you visualize both the story and the formula. If this story does not make sense to you, simply create your own using the same formulas. The idea is to find a way to remember all of the formulas in an easy-to-recall fashion.

The following chart may be helpful in understanding the formula descriptions.

Story Element	Formula Abbreviation	Formula Description	Formula
EXPERIMENTAL VEHICLE	EV	Earned Value (previously know as BCWP=Budgeted Cost of Work Performed)	EV = BAC * %COMP
BACK	BAC	Budget At Completion	
PERCENT COMPLETE	%COMP		
COMMERCIAL VEHICLES	CV	Cost Variance	CV = EV − AC
AIR CONDITIONING,	AC	Actual Costs (previously known as ACWP=Actual Cost of Work Performed)	
SPORT VEHICLE	SV	Schedule Variance	SV = EV − PV
PUBLIC VEHICLE	PV	Planned Value (previously known as BCWS=Budgeted Cost of Work Scheduled)	
CRASH POSITION INDICATOR	CPI	Cost Performance Index	CPI = EV / AC
SMART PLUG-INS	SPI	Schedule Performance Index	SPI = EV / PV
ELECTRONIC AIR CLEANER	EAC	Estimate At Completion	EAC = AC / %COMP
ENVIRONMENTAL TECHNOLOGY CENTER	ETC	Estimate To Complete	ETC = EAC − AC
VOLUNTARY ACTION COMMITTEE	VAC	Value At Completion	VAC = BAC − EAC

Remember, the point is to create a story that will help you recall the formulas. If the car industry story does not do it for you, create one that will. Some ideas might be: children's nursery rhymes, song titles, TV shows, movie titles, famous political figures or a funny story from your childhood.

To convert the story to the formulas and document the memory map, first start with the math symbols:

Build a warrior stick figure in 8 steps	
* (Head) - (1st Upper Appendage) - (2nd Upper Appendage) / (Shoulders) / (Side) / (Side) - (1st Lower Appendage) - (2nd Lower Appendage)	*

Use the stick figure as your mental reminder of the order of the math and then repeat the auto industry story using the formulas as your outline. It will be documented in the memory map like this:

⑨ Earned Value Analysis

EV = BAC * % Comp

CV = EV - AC

SV = EV - PV

CPI = EV / AC

SPI = EV / PV

EAC = AC / % Comp

ETC = EAC - AC

VAC = BAC - EAC

PRACTICE MAKES PERFECT!

Take time now to practicing your mapping techniques. Copy the above map over multiple times until you can recreate it without looking at it in the book or at the one you previously drew.

PRACTICE MAKES PERFECT!

Preparing for the Kickoff

Project managers are always looking for the checklist to make sure they are ready for their first Project Kickoff Meeting. Below is a diagram that is not only helpful to project managers, but is necessary to understand before taking the PMP® Exam. Study it carefully and make sure you can recreate it in record time. This diagram illustrates the inputs / outputs of the various processes from Project Charter to Project Plan Kickoff. It will be documented in the memory map as shown below.

10.)

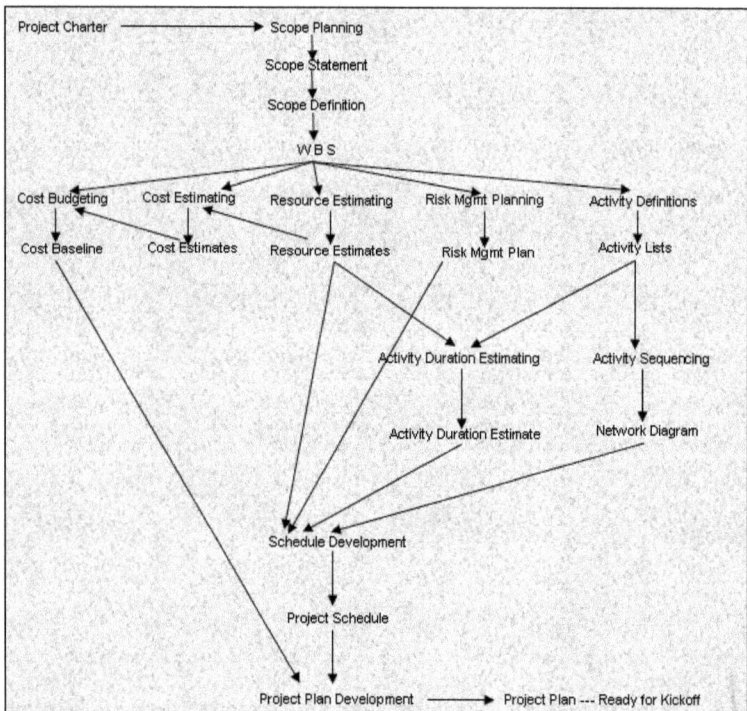

PRACTICE MAKES PERFECT!

Take time now to practicing your mapping techniques. Copy the above map over multiple times until you can recreate it without looking at it in the book or at the one you previously drew.

PRACTICE MAKES PERFECT!

Historic Data

The final portion of the memory map relates to historic data that is found in previous projects and can be beneficial to the current project. This is an acronym displayed as:

H I S T O R I C

The terms that follow are not necessarily logical, but the data represented is helpful.

The "H" represents the history that is gathered during the project plan development process. The "I" stands for the Initiating process where data from former projects is sought. The "S" is for the scope development process for the same reasons. The "T" represents Activity Sequencing and it is not known why it is signified by a "T"; we just accept it as so! Quantitative Risk Analysis is represented by the "O", possibly because it is close in visuals to a "Q". "R" is for resource planning and it is definitely helpful to refer back to projects of similar scope for guidance in determining the amount of resources that will be required. The "I" stands for identifying the risks and "C" is for cost estimates required in preparing the project plan.

The memory map will document the historic data as:

11.)

H	Proj Plan Dev
I	Initiating
S	Scope Dev
T	Act Seq
O	Quantitative Risk Analysis
R	Res Plan
I	Risk ID
C	Cost Est

PRACTICE MAKES PERFECT!

Take time now to practicing your mapping techniques. Copy the above map over multiple times until you can recreate it without looking at it in the book or at the one you previously drew.

PRACTICE MAKES PERFECT!

Putting the Pieces Together

To understand how the memory map works, you must first arrange the 11 charts into the following order on two pages (front and back of one sheet of 8.5 x 11 paper).

Front:

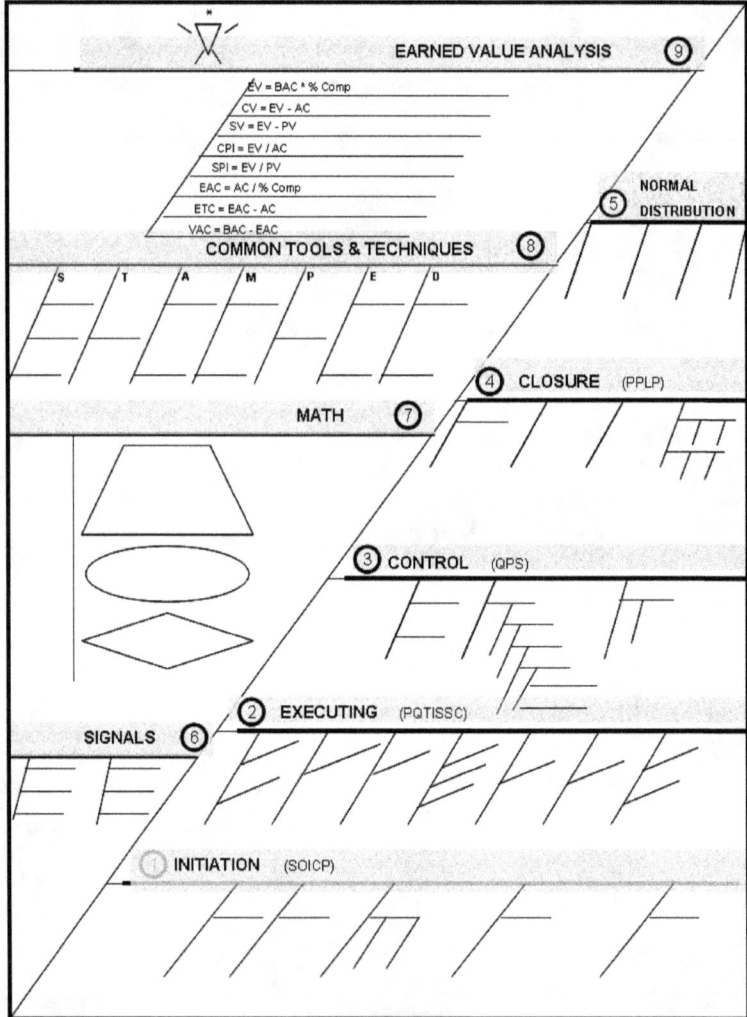

Back:

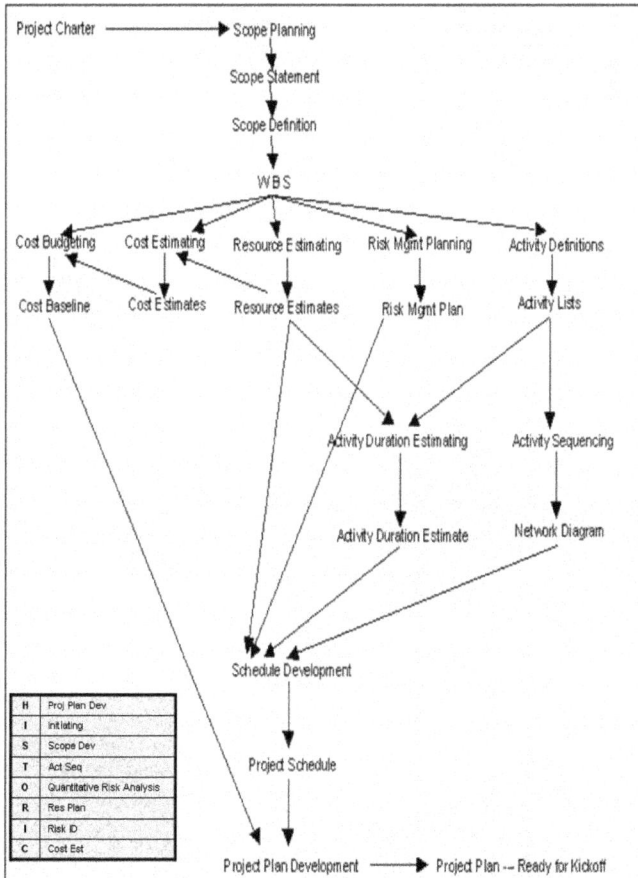

Once the charts have been copied to the paper, copy them over and over until you have them memorized. Once you have them locked into memory, begin racing the clock to make sure you can get the front and back completed within 5 minutes.

PRACTICE MAKES PERFECT!

PRACTICE MAKES PERFECT!

PRACTICE MAKES PERFECT!

PRACTICE MAKES PERFECT!

PRACTICE MAKES PERFECT!

Final Tips

As you are entering the testing center to take your exam, here are some tips to help make your experience a little easier:

1. **Remember to breath!** Don't hyperventilate. Take a moment and stretch your arms, your hands, your neck and relieve the tension.

2. **Take a break!** If you try to go from the beginning to the end without stopping, you are likely to get fatigued and miss easy questions. Pace yourself. There are 200 questions, you have four hours to complete the exam so a natural break is after every 50. Stand up, leave the testing area, get a drink of water and stretch.

3. **Read the questions carefully!** It is easy to assume you know the question without taking the time to read it thoroughly. Don't fall into this trap. It will save you a lot of frustration if you will slow down and read the question.

4. **Read all four answers!** Just as you might assume you know the question, don't assume you recognize the correct answer. Remember, there may be more than one right answer. Your task is to identify the MOST correct answer.

The PMP® Certification is a prestigious one and not one which you can come by easily. However, with the tips, tools, and techniques you will be on your way to successfully preparing for your exam. Remember, PRACTICE MAKES PERFECT!

Working with Teams and
Behaviors to Exemplify & Encourage

1. Help others be right, not wrong

2. Look for ways to make new ideas work, not for reasons why they won't

3. If in doubt, check it out; don't make assumptions about each other

4. Help each other win and take pride in others victories

5. Speak positively about each other and your organization, at every opportunity

6. Maintain a positive mental attitude no matter what the circumstances

7. Act with initiative and courage as it all depends on you

8. Do everything with enthusiasm

9. Whatever you want, give it away

10. Don't lose faith -- NEVER GIVE UP

Bibliography

A Guide to the Project Management Body of Knowledge: PMBOK Guide (2000 Edition). (2001). Newton Square, PA: Project Management Institute, Inc.

A Guide to the Project Management Body of Knowledge: PMBOK Guide (3rd Edition). (2004). Newton Square, PA: Project Management Institute, Inc.

Carter, Rita. (1998). Mapping the Mind. Los Angeles, CA: University of California Press

Nast, Jamie. (2001). *Idea Mapping: How to Access Your Hidden Brain Power, Learn Faster, Remember More, and Achieve Success in Business.* Hoboken, New Jersey: John Wiley & Sons, Inc.

Osmond, Joanne. (2005). *The Book Within You.* Lake Villa, IL: The Vision Tree, Ltd.

Bibliography

... Project Management Body of Knowledge ...
... Project Management Institute, Inc.

... Body of Knowledge (A Guide to the
Project Management Body of Knowledge)
Project Management Institute, Inc.

... (198) Managing the Mind ...
... Ann, CA, University of California Press.

... (200) Mike ... ... Press
... Plan Effort: Build Phases Begin Tasks ...
... ... Hoboken, New Jersey, John Wiley.

... ...
... ... the Virtual Desk.

The Vision Tree

The Vision Tree Services

The Vision Tree offers speaking engagements, workshop facilitation, and custom programs utilizing a variety of Business Survival games and workbooks.

Programs / Workshops

The Vision Tree provides business support for individuals who want to go into business for themselves. With years of personal experience and connections with the Business Development Center and Chambers of Commerce, we remain current in the trends that affect new businesses. The objective of our business programs is to help organizations achieve their vision by creating motivated individuals, productive teams, and high-performing organizations.

Business Survival Games

We facilitate innovative team-building activities using Insights programs and Survival games that are customized to quickly engage participants in internalizing best practices. Standard Business Survival games are available for: Customer Service, Sales, Information Technology, Manufacturing, Construction, Entrepreneurs, School Boards, and Not-for-Profit organizations. Games can also be customized for clients. "Business Survival in the BAG" is an alternative game used when there is less space, a larger audience, or less time. While not a Team-Building Event, it utilizes our Business Survival Cards from the Business Survival Games.

Insight Programs

The cornerstone of our communication workshops is the Insights Discovery Profile©. Team Building Profiles and 360 Assessments recognize diverse personalities and the contributions each employee makes to the team. More information is available at **www.TheVisionTree.com**.

Book Editing and Publishing

As a Small Press Publisher, The Vision Tree assists in publishing books either for the author to sell, to give to their clients, or to present as gifts to family and friends. Tools to help authors are available including research notebooks, books, templates, and editing services.

Professional Speaking Services

As a 20-year veteran in the speaking business, Joanne Osmond has addressed groups ranging from 15 to 1,500 (local school settings to international sites). She speaks on business survival, leadership styles, customer support, communication, and dealing with change. Her pragmatic advice includes not just the fluff but the nuts and bolts on how to make it happen. Her hallmark is the lasting value of what she presents.

To receive an information packet, call 847.833.2546 or E-mail **info@TheVisionTree.com**.

More Information

Call or E-mail today for more information on how we can enhance your team's performance. Your business survival is our business.

About the Author

Claudia Pannell is a business coach with The Vision Tree, Ltd. which helps clients address today's business challenges. Clients seeking assistance come from small, medium and large businesses and include individual owners to Fortune 500 management teams.

Prior to joining The Vision Tree, Ltd., Claudia spent the majority of her career at Abbott serving as a Computer Analyst, Project Leader, and Systems Manager. Additionally, she volunteered her time as a corporate mentor and Officer of the IT Women's Leadership Network.

Claudia offers her clients a wide range of programs and services including workshops for teambuilding, problem solving, project management and strategic planning. Most activities are designed to aid clients in identifying problem areas within their organization, analyzing potential solutions and developing manageable action plans to be implemented.

By specializing in the coaching of small groups, Claudia utilizes the techniques beneficial to effecting positive change and establishing continuous improvement for their organizations. She employs a variety of tools based on the client's environment and the time allowed.

After a successful career in IT Management, Claudia now coaches others to achieve the same success in their chosen fields. She derives much pleasure in seeing others overcome their barriers, face challenges in an affirmative manner and succeed in improving their organizations. This has led her to witness the positive growth of individuals as they achieve their own level of success.

As no stranger to the business environment, she spent a combined 25 years as a business professional for IBM, Kaiser Aluminum and as the owner of a retail lumber specialty company in North Texas prior to her retirement from Abbott. This has provided Claudia the foundation needed when addressing the ever-changing business environment.

In 2004, The Vision Tree started producing a series of Business Survival Games that are used in custom workshops that facilitate team building and internalize business best practices. Claudia Pannell and Joanne Osmond facilitate workshops using Insights programs and other unique tools that are truly remembered long after the event is over.

"Your workshop was the first in my entire life that really made me feel like I added value to the team."

Administrative Assistant

"For three months I have tried to break the ice with the team leaders without success. Today it happened in your workshop. It is a unique approach that really works."

Consultant

"I thought a team building activity was a dumb idea so I planned to sneak out as soon as I could. Did you notice that nobody left even to conduct business? It was fantastic, the best business event I have ever attended. Thanks!"

Project Manager

Contact **survival@TheVisionTree.com** for more information about customizing a game or to get assistance in publishing the book within you.

Our workshop and program information is available at **www.TheVisionTree.com** or readers can contact the staff at 847.833.2546.

Business Survival Games and Books
The Vision Tree, Ltd.
216 Waterbury Circle, Lake Villa, IL 60046
Survival@TheVisionTree.com
847.833.2546   Fax: 847.356.3783

	Unit Price	Number Ordered	Sub Total
Business Survival Workbooks With CD			
Are You Ready?	24.99		
Business Survival	24.99		
Business Survival Workshops / Team Building			
Custom Business Survival Program	5% Discount - Call for detail		
Business Survival for Authors			
The Book Within You	15.99		
The Book's in the Bag includes Book	24.99		
Business Survival Games			
Student Version	24.99		
Customer Service Version	24.99		
Entrepreneurial Version	24.99		
Small Business Version	24.99		
Project Management Version	24.99		
Insights Version	24.99		
Other _____	24.99		

Note: Volume Discounts Available

Total Product	
9% Handling, Tax, Shipping	
Total Order	

Name _____

Address _____

City, State, Zip _____

Phone _____

E-mail address _____

Credit Card Information   Visa   Mastercard   Discover

Name on Card _____

Credit Card Number _____

Expiration Date _____

Security Code _____

Signature _____

www.ingramcontent.com/pod-product-compliance
Lightning Source LLC
Chambersburg PA
CBHW071116210326
41519CB00020B/6322